Step 1
Go to www.openlightbox.com

Step 2
Enter this unique code
NOLBW4UTB

Step 3
Explore your interactive eBook!

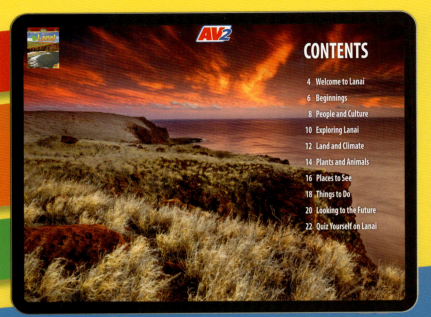

CONTENTS

4 Welcome to Lanai
6 Beginnings
8 People and Culture
10 Exploring Lanai
12 Land and Climate
14 Plants and Animals
16 Places to See
18 Things to Do
20 Looking to the Future
22 Quiz Yourself on Lanai

AV2 is optimized for use on any device

Your interactive eBook comes with...

Contents
Browse a live contents page to easily navigate through resources

Audio
Listen to sections of the book read aloud

Videos
Watch informative video clips

Weblinks
Gain additional information for research

Slideshows
View images and captions

Try This!
Complete activities and hands-on experiments

Key Words
Study vocabulary, and complete a matching word activity

Quizzes
Test your knowledge

Share
Share titles within your Learning Management System (LMS) or Library Circulation System

Citation
Create bibliographical references following APA, CMOS, and MLA styles

This title is part of our AV2 digital subscription

1-Year Grades K–5 Subscription
ISBN 978-1-7911-3320-7

Access hundreds of AV2 titles with our digital subscription.
Sign up for a FREE trial at www.openlightbox.com/trial

The digital components of this book are guaranteed to stay active for at least five years from the date of publication.

Lanai
"The Pineapple Isle"

CONTENTS
- 2   Interactive eBook Code
- 4   Welcome to Lanai
- 6   Beginnings
- 8   People and Culture
- 10   Exploring Lanai
- 12   Land and Climate
- 14   Plants and Animals
- 16   Places to See
- 18   Things to Do
- 20   Looking to the Future
- 22   Quiz Yourself on Lanai
- 23   Key Words/Index

LANAI—The Pineapple Isle

WELCOME TO Lanai

- Lanai is the **smallest** of all the **inhabited** Hawaiian Islands.
- Lanai receives approximately **100,000 visitors** annually.
- Lanai has only about **30 miles** (48 kilometers) of paved road and **no traffic lights**.

Aloha! Welcome to Lanai! Lanai is part of the Hawaiian Islands, an **archipelago** in the central Pacific Ocean. This archipelago makes up the U.S. state of Hawaii. Lanai is the sixth largest Hawaiian Island. The archipelago itself has more than 130 islands. Lanai's closest neighbors are the islands of Maui, Kahoolawe, and Molokai.

Lanai is often called "The Pineapple Isle." This is because it was once home to the world's largest pineapple **plantation**. At one time, this plantation produced close to 75 percent of the world's pineapples.

THE ISLAND OF Lanai

Population: 3,200 (2024)

Area: 140 square miles (363 square km)

Altitude: 3,370 feet (1,027 meters) at its highest point

County Seat: Wailuku, Maui County

Island Flower: Kaunaoa

Island Color: Orange

LANAI—The Pineapple Isle

Beginnings

Following the arrival of its initial settlers, Lanai became a center for inter-island trade.

The Hawaiian Islands began to develop approximately 6 million years ago. They were formed by volcanic activity that occurred deep underground. Lanai is believed to be about 1.3 million years old.

The first people to live on Lanai were **Polynesians** who had already settled on two other Hawaiian Islands, Molokai and Kahoolawe. They arrived on Lanai more than 800 years ago. These settlers established small fishing villages along the coast. Shortly after, they moved into Lanai's interior, where they grew **taro** in the fertile volcanic soil.

The first European to see Lanai was Captain Charles Clerke, on February 25, 1779. In 1922, James Dole, the president of the Hawaiian Pineapple Company, bought the entire island of Lanai. He turned a large portion of the land into a pineapple plantation.

Lanai's pineapple plantation era thrived for about 70 years. It came to an end due mainly to increased global competition.

Speaking Hawaiian

The word *Lanai* is pronounced "la-NAH-ee." It means "day of conquest." The name is related to a prince named Kaululaau, who is believed to have driven all the evil spirits from the island.

6 HAWAII

Lanai Timeline

1200s
Native Hawaiians begin to settle on Lanai.

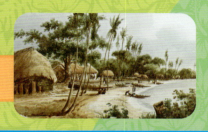

Late 1700s
As part of his campaign to rule over the Hawaiian Islands, King Kamehameha I takes control of Lanai.

1861
Walter Murray Gibson arrives on Lanai to organize a **colony** on behalf of the Church of Jesus Christ of Latter-day Saints. He later establishes a large sheep ranching operation on the island.

1922
James Dole purchases Lanai for $1.1 million.

1959
Lanai becomes part of Maui County when Hawaii is admitted into the United States.

2012
Billionaire Larry Ellison buys 98 percent of Lanai for $300 million.

2024
A new proposal for expanding **ferry** service between the islands of Lanai, Maui, and Molokai is put forward to the local government.

LANAI—The Pineapple Isle

People and Culture

Lanai has undergone several changes throughout its history. From early Polynesian fishing villages to ranches and a pineapple plantation, each development has brought new people and new **traditions** to the island. Lanai's cultural makeup is now a blend of Hawaiian, Chinese, Japanese, Filipino, Spanish, and Portuguese influences. Still, it is the traditions of the original Polynesian settlers that remain at the core of Lanai culture.

One such tradition is the luau. In the past, ancient Hawaiians held these large feasts to commemorate events such as a victory at battle or a successful harvest. Today, they are a way to celebrate weddings, births, and other special occasions. Some luaus are also staged solely for the tourists that visit the island.

The start of a luau is often announced by the trumpeting of a conch shell.

Speaking Hawaiian

In Hawaiian, *luau* means "banquet" or "feast." It is pronounced "LOO-ow."

8 HAWAII

Music and dance are a big part of any luau. Guests are treated to the sounds of traditional drums and rattles, as well as the fluid movements of the hula dance. They often dine on traditional Hawaiian foods such as kalua pork and poi. The food is typically eaten at a low table covered in **ti** leaves and decorated with flowers and fruit. The luau may close with the telling of local legends. In Lanai, many of these stories explain the significance of certain landmarks found on the island.

The traditional way to make kalua pork is by cooking it in an underground oven called an imu.

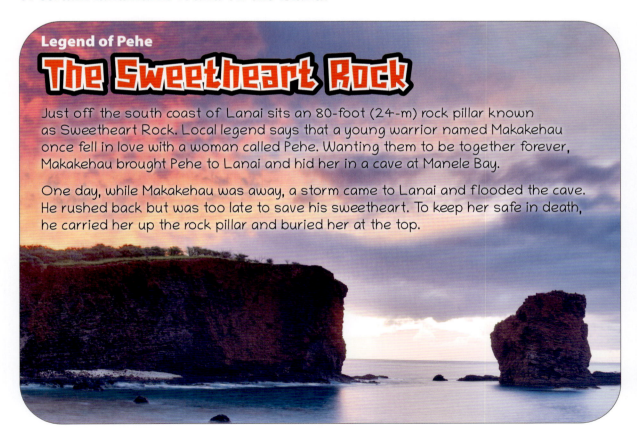

Legend of Pehe
The Sweetheart Rock

Just off the south coast of Lanai sits an 80-foot (24-m) rock pillar known as Sweetheart Rock. Local legend says that a young warrior named Makakehau once fell in love with a woman called Pehe. Wanting them to be together forever, Makakehau brought Pehe to Lanai and hid her in a cave at Manele Bay.

One day, while Makakehau was away, a storm came to Lanai and flooded the cave. He rushed back but was too late to save his sweetheart. To keep her safe in death, he carried her up the rock pillar and buried her at the top.

LANAI—The Pineapple Isle

Exploring Lanai

Lanai is located almost in the middle of the Hawaiian Islands. It is shaped like an apostrophe. Even though Lanai is small, it has a variety of features. These include white sand beaches, a **rainforest**, and a volcanic mountain.

Lanai City

Most of Lanai's population is found in and around Lanai City, in the center of the island. Established by James Dole in the early 1920s, Lanai City is known for its historic buildings and Dole Park, a gathering place in the heart of the town.

Garden of the Gods

Garden of the Gods is a desert-like area in the island's northwest. With virtually no plant life, the garden is known for its rock towers, spires, and scattered boulders.

Lanaihale

At more than 3,300 feet (1,000 m) in elevation, Lanaihale is Lanai's highest peak. It is also a volcano, although long **extinct**. Lanaihale last erupted about 1.2 million years ago.

Shipwreck Beach

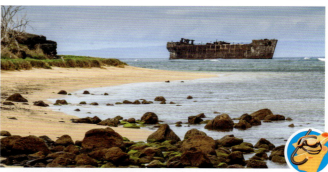

At the north end of Lanai is an 8-mile (13-km) stretch of coast known as Shipwreck Beach. The remains of at least a dozen ships, ranging from oil tankers to World War II vessels, can be viewed here.

HAWAII

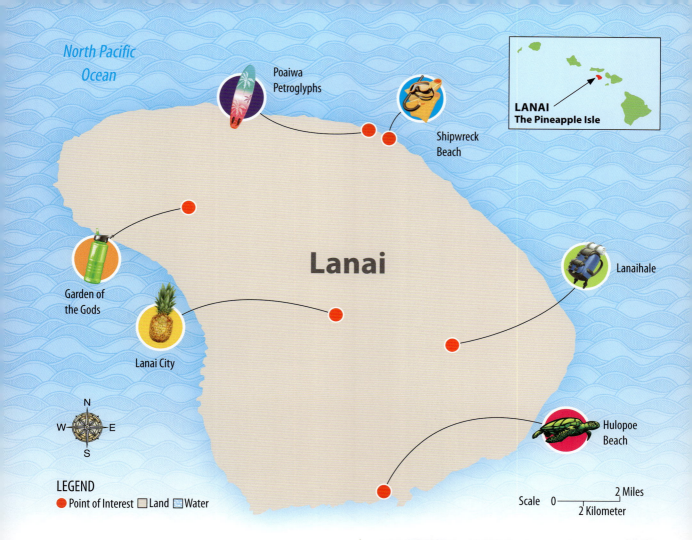

Poaiwa Petroglyphs

The Poaiwa **petroglyphs** are located a short distance from Shipwreck Beach. Hundreds of years old, these rock carvings provide insight into the island's past. One depicts a hunting scene. Others show people surfing and fishing.

Hulopoe Beach

Hulopoe Beach is Lanai's most popular swimming spot. Its waves and winds are usually low. The clear waters make it a good place for snorkeling. Visitors might even encounter sea turtles or dolphins while swimming.

LANAI—The Pineapple Isle

Land and Climate

Most of Lanai's landscape is rugged, with craggy cliffs, rolling hills, and rocky shores. Although the island has 47 miles (76 km) of coastline, only its southern coast offers an easily accessible beach. Pristine white sand and crystal blue waters are the main features of this area. There are no rivers or lakes on the island.

At the center of Lanai is a plateau. This flat, elevated area rises sharply from its surroundings and is almost 1,700 feet (518 m) above sea level. Lanai City is located here.

Found on Lanai's north shore, Polihua Beach stretches more than 1.5 miles (2.4 km), making it the island's longest white-sand beach.

Speaking Hawaiian

The word **Lanaihale**, pronounced "**la-NA-ya-ha-lay**," means "**House of Lanai**."

12 HAWAII

Lanai's **climate** is cool when compared to the other Hawaiian Islands. Temperatures range from 61 to 81 degrees Fahrenheit (16 to 27 degrees Celsius), with July through October being the hottest months. The warmest areas are along the beaches. The coolest temperatures are found at the peak of Lanaihale. While some of the Hawaiian Islands can receive significant rainfall, Lanai is drier. It averages less than 40 inches (102 centimeters) annually. Most of the island's rain falls between the months of November and March.

Average High Temperatures	
JAN	73°F (23°C)
FEB	73°F (23°C)
MAR	75°F (24°C)
APR	75°F (24°C)
MAY	75°F (24°C)
JUN	77°F (25°C)
JUL	79°F (26°C)
AUG	79°F (26°C)
SEP	81°F (27°C)
OCT	79°F (26°C)
NOV	77°F (25°C)
DEC	75°F (24°C)

To compensate for lower rainfall levels, Lanai's plants take in moisture from low-hanging clouds. It sinks into the ground, providing the plants with the water they need to grow.

LANAI—The Pineapple Isle

Plants and Animals

Lanai is home to many different plants and animals. The island is well known for its abundance of flowers. Its waters have many types of sea life, and its land is full of native birds.

Spinner Dolphin

Spinner dolphins can often be seen in the waters off Lanai's Hulopoe Bay. These small dolphins are named for their ability to leap and spin out of the water. They can spin in the air up to seven times before falling back into the water.

Lanai Tree Snail

The Lanai tree snail is found only on the island of Lanai, where it lives in the wet forests and surrounding cliffs. There, it feeds on **microorganisms** that live on leaves and other plant matter. This snail is considered **endangered**, due mainly to predators and human development.

HAWAII

Chital

Lanai is home to the highest **density** of free-roaming chital, or axis deer, in the world, with an estimated 25,000 on the island. The deer were brought to the Hawaiian Islands from India in 1867 as a gift to the king. A small herd was moved to Lanai in 1920. With no predators on the island, the population has continued to grow.

Kanawao

Kanawao is **endemic** to six of the Hawaiian Islands, including Lanai. This shrub is typically found in forested areas at high elevations and prefers a wet environment. Its blooms can be white, yellow, pink, blue, green, or purple. Happy-faced spiders can often be found hanging from its leaves.

Pueo

Also known as the Hawaiian short-eared owl, this bird is the only owl endemic to the archipelago. It can be found on Lanai and the other main islands. Unlike most owls, the pueo hunts during the day. It often searches open areas for mice, insects, and other birds.

Lele

Lele thrives in the moist environment of Lanai's rainforests. As a climbing plant, it can often be found growing up tree trunks and rock faces. Historically, the plant had many uses. As a medicine, it helped to bring on sleep. Early Hawaiians also used it to make fishing nets and lines.

LANAI—The Pineapple Isle

Places to See

People wanting to visit Lanai can do so using inter-island airlines or ferries.

As one of the least populated Hawaiian Islands, Lanai offers visitors a more laid-back tourist experience. There are rarely crowds, which leaves people more room to roam. The island still has many places to see and experience. These range from natural landmarks to cultural and historical sites.

The fishing village of Kaunolu is a U.S. National Historic Landmark. It was a favorite fishing spot of King Kamehameha I. Abandoned in the 1880s, Kaunolu is now the largest surviving ruin of a prehistoric Hawaiian village in the entire archipelago. Visitors can see petroglyphs, the remains of a sacred temple, and "Kahekili's Leap," a 60-foot (18-m) cliff where warriors demonstrated their bravery by diving into the water below.

Kaunolu is both historic and scenic, providing expansive views of Lanai's southern sea cliffs.

The Lanai Culture & Heritage Center is a museum in Lanai City. Visitors can learn about Lanai's Hawaiian heritage, its culture, and the history of the ranching and plantation eras of the island. The museum offers two main exhibits, as well as virtual exhibits. Archives containing more than 40,000 items help tell the story of Lanai and the many people who have called the island home.

Some of the artifacts on display at the Lanai Culture & Heritage Center date back almost 1,000 years.

Open since 2004, the Lanai Cat Sanctuary is currently home to more than 600 rescue cats. The sanctuary believes that all cats deserve to live their best possible life. Many of the sanctuary's residents are **feral** cats that were living in areas where native and endangered ground-nesting birds also lived. To ensure the safety of both types of animals, the cats were removed and taken to the sanctuary. Open 365 days a year, people are welcome to visit the cats, work as volunteers, and donate money and supplies. The sanctuary also offers an adoption program for people wanting a cat of their own.

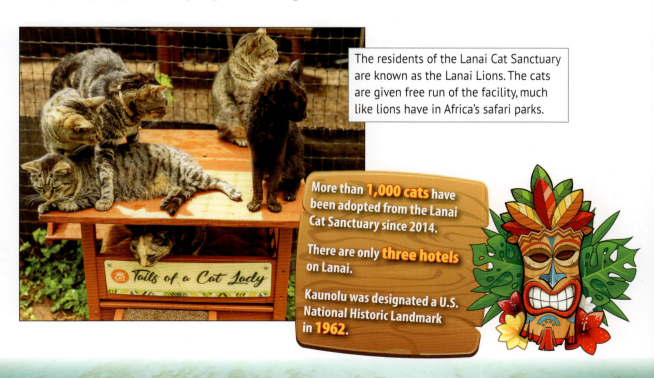

The residents of the Lanai Cat Sanctuary are known as the Lanai Lions. The cats are given free run of the facility, much like lions have in Africa's safari parks.

More than **1,000 cats** have been adopted from the Lanai Cat Sanctuary since 2014.

There are only **three hotels** on Lanai.

Kaunolu was designated a U.S. National Historic Landmark in **1962**.

LANAI—The Pineapple Isle

Things to Do

Lanai is often said to have some of the Hawaiian Islands' best hiking trails. One of the most popular is Munro Trail, a 13-mile (21-km) climb that takes hikers up to the summit of Lanaihale. On the way, they travel through the island's rainforest and take in stunning canyon views of Manalei Gulch. Upon reaching the summit, it is possible to see all six major Hawaiian Islands if the skies are clear.

One of Lanai's easier hikes can be done at Garden of the Gods. The trail is more than 1 mile (1.6 km) long and takes about 2 hours to complete.

Off-roading is an activity that lets visitors explore Lanai to its fullest. With most of the island's roads unpaved, having a four-wheel drive vehicle gives visitors access to some of the island's best-known sites, including Shipwreck Beach and Garden of the Gods. They can also forge their own path to parts of the island few others ever see.

Lanai has about 400 miles (644 km) of unpaved road for people to explore via an off-road vehicle.

18 HAWAII

Many people come to Lanai for its scuba diving opportunities. There are more than 13 dive sites around the island. The dives range from 30 to 80 feet (9 to 24 m) deep. Experienced divers often explore the Lanai Cathedrals. This dive site features two large caverns that were created from **lava tubes**.

Divers can encounter a wide variety of sea creatures, ranging from tropical fish to sea turtles, inside the Lanai Cathedrals.

Humpback whales can be seen around all of the Hawaiian Islands, but the Auau Channel, between Lanai, Maui, and Molokai, is one of the world's best whale-watching spots. People may see whales spouting or breaching from the coast or during a ferry ride between Lanai and Maui. However, the best way to see whales is on a tour. Marine naturalist guides are typically onboard to teach visitors about sea life. Many of the boats are also equipped with hydrophones. These microphones allow visitors to listen to the underwater sounds of the whales.

Humpback whales begin to arrive in Lanai's waters in the fall, but the best time to see them in great quantity is February.

LANAI—The Pineapple Isle

Looking to the Future

As an island, Lanai has a unique **ecosystem**, with life forms that are found nowhere else in the world. Many of these organisms are in jeopardy of disappearing due to a variety of issues, ranging from **climate change** to land development. One of the main culprits, however, is the arrival of **invasive species** on the island. Axis deer, domestic cats, and many other animals have been brought to Lanai from other places. These animals eat Lanai's plants, taking food away from native animals. Some even use the native animals as food. Populations of several native plants and animals are falling as a result.

The people of Lanai are working to reduce the impact of these invasive species. The Lanai Cat Sanctuary is one example of how invasive animal species are being removed from areas they can harm. Efforts have also been made to remove invasive plant species so that native species have more room to grow and flourish.

The Hawaiian petrel is now endangered in Hawaii due partially to invasive species, such as cats and mongooses, feeding on its eggs. On Lanai, these birds are restricted to the higher elevations of Lanaihale.

Speaking Hawaiian

Lanai is known for its *ohana*, pronounced "o-HA-na." The Hawaiian word for "family," ohana signifies the small-town feel and sense of community found on the island.

20 HAWAII

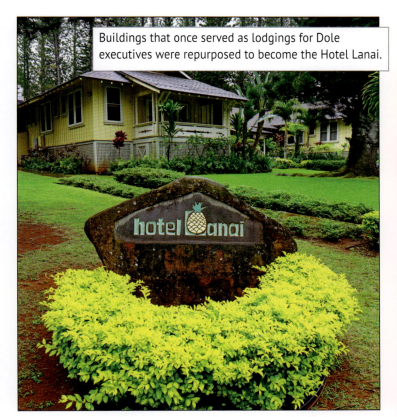

Buildings that once served as lodgings for Dole executives were repurposed to become the Hotel Lanai.

Lanai's population is also facing its challenges. The island has an aging **infrastructure** and is in need of an updated waterworks system and new housing developments. At the same time, islanders do not want Lanai to lose its small-town personality. Some of the island's old plantation homes have already been demolished to make way for new buildings. There is fear that the historic elements of the island may be lost over time.

Plans are currently underway to upgrade the water supply system on the island. Local officials are also looking at how to restore or repurpose some of Lanai's historic buildings. The hope is that new construction can be added in a way that does not detract from the island's charm.

SPOTLIGHT on CHANGE

The Lanai Culture & Heritage Center hosts an annual Kupulau Festival. The festival is held to celebrate the volunteer work done to care for the island. Educational booths and interactive crafts provide opportunities for people to learn about the important conservation work happening on Lanai. Free native plants are given out for people to plant in their gardens. Do you think this educational festival is a good way to preserve the history and culture of Lanai? What else could be done?

LANAI—The Pineapple Isle

QUIZ YOURSELF ON Lanai

1. How many traffic lights does Lanai have?

2. Why is Lanai known as "The Pineapple Isle"?

3. How many rescue cats are housed at the Lanai Cat Sanctuary?

4. Who was the first European to see Lanai?

5. How tall is Sweetheart Rock?

6. What is the name of Lanai's highest peak?

7. What does *luau* mean?

8. Which Lanai village was a favorite fishing spot of King Kamehameha I?

ANSWERS: 1. None **2.** It was once home to a plantation that produced 75 percent of the world's pineapples. **3.** More than 600 **4.** Captain Charles Clerke **5.** 80 feet (24 m) **6.** Lanaihale **7.** "Banquet" or "feast" **8.** Kaunolu

22 HAWAII

Key Words

archipelago: a group of islands

climate: the average weather conditions of a particular place or region over a period of years

climate change: long-lasting changes to Earth's weather patterns

colony: an area subject to a form of foreign rule

density: the concentration of individuals within a specific area

ecosystem: a community of living organisms in a particular area

endangered: in danger of no longer living on Earth

endemic: native and restricted to a certain place

extinct: no longer active

feral: wild but descended from domestic animals

ferry: a boat used to carry passengers, vehicles, or goods

infrastructure: the basic facilities and systems serving a country, city, or area, such as transportation, power plants, and schools

invasive species: an introduced species that harms its new environment

lava tubes: underground passageways created by lava flows

microorganisms: any living things too small to be viewed by the unaided eye

petroglyphs: ancient rock carvings

plantation: an agricultural estate worked by laborers

Polynesians: Indigenous people who come from the islands of Polynesia

rainforest: dense forests that receive heavy annual rainfall and are made up of tall evergreen trees whose tops form a continuous layer

taro: a large-leaved plant grown for its edible, starchy, underground stem

ti: a flowering shrub that native Hawaiians used to make items such as clothing, food, and fishing equipment

traditions: information, beliefs, or customs handed down from one generation to another

animals 11, 14, 15, 17, 19, 20

Clerke, Captain Charles 6, 22
climate 12, 13, 20

Dole, James 6, 7, 10

Garden of the Gods 10, 11, 18

Hawaiian Pineapple Company 6
hiking 18
hula dance 9
Hulopoe Beach 11

infrastructure 21
invasive species 20

Kamehameha I, King 7, 16, 22
Kaunolu 16, 17, 22

Lanai Cat Sanctuary 17, 20, 22
Lanai City 10, 11, 12, 17
Lanai Culture & Heritage Center 17, 21
Lanaihale 10, 11, 12, 13, 18, 20, 22
luau 8, 9, 22

Munro Trail 18

off-roading 18

plantation 5, 6, 8, 17, 21, 22
plants 13, 14, 15, 20, 21
Poaiwa petroglyphs 11
Polynesians 6, 8

scuba diving 19
Shipwreck Beach 10, 11, 18
Sweetheart Rock 9, 22

volcano 6, 10

whale watching 19

LANAI—The Pineapple Isle 23

Get the best of both worlds.

AV2 bridges the gap between print and digital.

The expandable resources toolbar enables quick access to content including **videos**, **audio**, **activities**, **weblinks**, **slideshows**, **quizzes**, and **key words**.

Animated videos make static images come alive.

Resource icons on each page help readers to further **explore key concepts**.

Published by Lightbox Learning Inc.
276 5th Avenue
Suite 704 #917
New York, NY 10001
Website: www.openlightbox.com

Copyright ©2026 Lightbox Learning Inc.
All rights reserved. No part of this publication may be reproduced, stored in a retrieval system, or transmitted in any form or by any means, electronic, mechanical, photocopying, recording, or otherwise, without the prior written permission of the publisher.

Library of Congress Cataloging-in-Publication Data

Names: Letkeman, Candice, author.
Title: Lanai "the Pineapple Isle" / Candice Letkeman.
Description: New York, NY : Lightbox Learning Inc., 2026. | Series: Hawaii | Includes index. | Audience: Grades 2-3
Identifiers: LCCN 2024047332 (print) | LCCN 2024047333 (ebook) | ISBN 9798874506629 (library binding) | ISBN 9798874506636 (paperback) | ISBN 9798874507480 (ebook other) | ISBN 9798874506643 (ebook other)
Subjects: LCSH: Lanai (Hawaii)--Juvenile literature.
Classification: LCC DU628.L3 L47 2026 (print) | LCC DU628.L3 (ebook) | DDC 919.69/23--dc23/eng/20241211
LC record available at https://lccn.loc.gov/2024047332
LC ebook record available at https://lccn.loc.gov/2024047333

Printed in Guangzhou, China
1 2 3 4 5 6 7 8 9 0 28 27 26 25 24

122024
101124

Project Coordinator: Heather Kissock
Designer: Terry Paulhus

Photo Credits
Every reasonable effort has been made to trace ownership and to obtain permission to reprint copyright material. The publisher would be pleased to have any errors or omissions brought to its attention so that they may be corrected in subsequent printings. The publisher acknowledges Getty Images, Alamy, Bridgeman Images, Shutterstock, and Wikimedia as its image suppliers for this title.

View new titles and product videos at **www.openlightbox.com**